PHILIP BENTALL

Where cows are met

Where cows are met

poems©Philip Bentall

First Edition 2019
ISBN: 978-1-907435-82-9

Published by Dempsey & Windle
15 Rosetrees
Guildford
Surrey
GU1 2HS
UK
01483 571164
dempseyandwindle.co.uk

Printed in England by BookPrintingUK, Peterborough

Cover picture from a painting by Janice Dempsey

A CIP record for this book can be obtained from the British Library

Contents

Where cows are met

Downland. A chalky emulsion
of trodden plantain and jutting flint
makes up its ridgeway track.
Overhead, skylarks' faint
invisible chirrup follows
in a dry verge hiss of wind,
wire-strummed.

An hour could be a year,
no one is seen.
Then, where the ground levels and falls away,
cows are met —
sleepy heads dip and dark eyes peer,
as if the last passer-by
wore skins and carried a flint-headed axe.

Time steams
and swirls off their mud-splattered hinds,
nostrils flare and sniff,
legs bend and brace.

Then the skittish backward lurch,
the startled-eyed retreat,
the avalanche of fears,

and the field explodes with hooves,
as if mallets of Stone Age fists
were set hammering in barrows under chalk.

The Farmyard

In barn shadow,
two collared doves scare
from a bank of corn.

Across a concrete expanse,
rivulets of manure
pool at a drain.

No one is about.
The metronome clinking of an iron gate;
a telegraph wire swings
like an abandoned skipping rope.

In the early chill,
the prehistoric bellow of a cow;
the slow wide eyes
through wooden slats.

From last night,
a calf lies dead on a sack;
its oversized tongue gripped in teeth and legs
folded back.

Beyond, tractor tracks
lead to silage bays,
where tarpaulin flaps
and sparrows scatter like loose shot.

Cows at the water trough

The tank slop
and ballcock hiss,
the rough tongue rubber
on galvanised metal —

cows jostle,
rub heads,
bulked with grass,
suctioned in mud.

A moment of stares,
head shakes
and mud-caked
tail flicks,

when bellows
unroll across fields
as slow as
the drift of continents.

He had no plans

I didn't know him well.
We worked together on a game farm one summer.
He liked Oasis,
Golden Virginia roll-ups,
Strongbow cider.

He lived at home,
took summer jobs,
slept late,
worried his mother.

Before the game farm,
car valets at a garage;
even he admitted,
beyond a wish to see Oasis at Wembley,
he had no plans.

He worked hard —
your heart went out to him,
built like a child's drawing,
stick-armed, badly proportioned.

When the season ended,
I gave him a lift home —
an epileptic, he didn't drive.
See you next year, I said.
He agreed.

The months passed.
It seems naïve now
to have taken him at his word.
But who was to know?

His father, poor sod,
the one to find him —
down on the family farm,
rope round his neck,
no note.

Chanctonbury Ring

Turf-sponge scalped to chalk,
trees adrift in mist, the ground
rising to a world-edge scarp face.

You remember the saying,
Run seven times around the ring
and the devil will take your soul.

A gate latch clinks
sacrificial tolls in the wind;
pigeons clatter from treetops;

flints roll underfoot —
tooth-chips spat out
from neolithic grins.

Mole

The blind paddle
through the chalk rendzina,

the bore-head spit
of flint

and uplift
of turf sponge,

the pocket-sized
borer

in this, its compressed solitude,
night after night —

forward thrust, backfill —
velvet-suited, aerial-tailed,

wired to magnetic fields —
ordained labourer,

earth shoveller,
worm guzzler —

the moon probably
just another bone to you —

as earth snout,
paddle mitts,

periscope through
to the other world.

The big bend

The river was at its widest here.
Beds of lilies and bulrushes
enclosed its far bank,
enticing us to see how far
we dared cast.

At first, content with numbers
not size, we filled our keep-nets
with rudd and roach.
Then came my first bream.
Its weight was like nothing else.
I felt my rod tip plunge as I struck.
And although it gave up the fight
with surprising ease, turning over at the surface
like a large dinner plate, its sheer size
was breathtaking.

Going deeper, we learnt to ledger
and hooked into eels,
the riverbed's live mud-sunken wires,
dragging them up from the shadows,
as they threshed expertly.
Then when we found someone
who'd pay us for them
we cut off their heads, coiled them up
in old ice cream containers,
and put them in our mothers' freezers.

With every catch
a step into the unknown,
we worked our way up

through the ranks of specimens:
from early morning bouts
wrestling tench,
to strong-arming carp at dusk.
In winter, with water freezing
in our rod eyes,
we dead-baited for pike.

I saw my first kingfisher here,
its bullet-flat trajectory mirrored on the water,
and cast into dawn mists,
the riverbanks armed with herons;
even drank my first can of beer here.

Ground elder

Kneeling to dig you out,
my thumb joints ache
gripping trowel and ripping
at your stems.

Your rhizomes, cemented in clay,
snap easily.
I sift for remains —
winning for now, I think.

But you'll be back, I know,
bursting through,
your shiny lobe-leafed progeny
full of the vigour of youth;

and although I'll take to
my knees again and continue
to maim your offspring — I also know,
in the end, you'll win.

Bird's nest

Strimming brambles
between a fence and ditch,
I spot a nest and stop.

The nest is old, dry but
still perfectly formed, moss lines its walls.
I look inside,

and what looks like
a fluff of wool —
turns out to be a skeleton,

minute boned, squat,
not much larger
than a thumbnail —

a chick, I guess,
whose mother
never came back.

Clem's shed

The ditch needed building up
where the cattle had trodden it in —
a mudslide of clay, cratered with hoof-prints,
dammed up the waterway.

A friend brought a trailer load
of hardcore round
and tipped it up onto the bank.
I watched, holding a shovel —

broken bricks,
with plaster still attached,
lumps of concrete, roof tiles.
Getting out the cab, my friend said, 'Clem's shed.'

Clem I knew from the shoot.
He drove the beaters' cart,
suffered with a hernia
and had recently moved — hence the shed.

'Yeah?' I answered.
The hardcore personalised
in a way I wouldn't have thought possible:
Clem part of the ground now.

12 Burghley Road

I

You were ninety-two this year,
while I was twenty-six,
four years since I answered your advert
in a newsagent's in Kentish Town.
Help needed, it read,
and your name: Ivy Stanton.
An interview followed — no mention
of CVs or experience.
I had a kind face, you said.
I got the job.

So a gardener I became
to old roses, dahlias and peonies,
in your garden with the air-raid shelter
your brother built before the war —
you came here in 1932,
had copper baths by the fire —
but we go back even further:
to your father's shop,
with the chocolates below the counter,
your brother's horses kept for deliveries,
and the boy on a bicycle
ringing a bell before air raids,
to the time you bought oranges
with your father's tobacco money
and got into trouble at school
when you tried to peel one in class.

Well, last week, on Saturday, a neighbour
found you lying unconscious on your kitchen floor
and you were taken to hospital.
The unkindness of old age, I thought.
You should be made like a cathedral
with all that's inside you.

You were frail, they said.
It seemed hardly accurate.
Your many faces played before me:
the girl called Ivy, skipping
down the Prince of Wales Road amid
the cobblestone clatter, steam and snort of horses,
the Ivy peeling oranges in class,
coming home late from school
and putting your father's chickens to bed,
to the young woman of shorthand,
French speaking, with a pound a week in wages,
who played tennis with a doctor in Croydon,
and took shelter down the Northern Line,
when London shouted, '*we can take it!*'

I came to see the old lady
I sat with at coffee time and called Mrs Stanton.
You're making jokes about running for Council
and winning a lottery million.
I recall your gentle, mischievous laugh
and Silver Jubilee biscuit tin.
Outside, in the shade of a buddleia,
pigeons share in your leftover meals.
The squirrels you feed at your door

are waiting for me to leave.
Next door's cat sits on your chair sleeping.
All life it seems surrounds you.

Get well soon, Mrs Stanton.
You gave me the gift of your life
at ninety-two, 12 Burghley Road.
I will never forget.
Last year, the Victoria plum tree
produced fifty-four pounds of fruit.
You called it its swan song, with
all its dead and creaking limbs,
only this year it produced sixty-one.

II

Ninety-three, ninety-four
I was never quite sure how old you were,
but always the same fond reminder
as we were saying goodbye
that you may not be here when roses bloomed next year,
but always you were
so that I never quite believed you'd go.

Well, this year it happened.
Seriously ill, they said.
You wouldn't be coming home.
How hospital never suited you.

I think of the roses I never got round to prune,
the buddleia will be all right, of course,
the daffs will be out.
Lioness of Burghley Road
I think of you alone, tiny-boned,
in a cold hospital bed,
time passing like a winter's afternoon.

I think of your husband, long dead, but closer now.
Reg, I hear you say
(he was a toolmaker before the War)
and your eyes twinkle
telling me how
you brought home a little more.
What a mischievous bride you must have been.
Reg died in 1933,
two years after you were married.
The love of your life, you said.

So, I think of you now —
not frail, alone, seriously ill —
but moving back then,
as in that photo on your shelf,
in which your clutching your husband's arm,
as you walk along Weymouth Beach,
your head turned to his,
the sea-breeze rippling your dress,
as if you were about to dance.

Black Poplar

It was by far the tallest tree in the garden,
had a cathedral presence,
with a girth you couldn't get your arms around,
bark, like the skin of an overripe fig,
split open in places, and leaves
that found a breeze —
with cooling twists —
even when there wasn't one.

It drew birds throughout the day:
crows cawed out their territory from it;
wood pigeons rested there between feeds;
while starlings, iridescent, garbled
into the evenings from its sun-tipped crown.
Then in summer, its cotton-wool like seeds
covered the garden in a snow
that never melted.

There were the injuries of course.
A branch snapped off
in the '87 gale, revealing
the surprising paleness of the wood inside,
but it soon recovered;
and from the crook
of the splintered stump
outthrust a new limb.

Scots Pine

Armour-plated,
mollusc-flaked,
clad for rocky outcrops and hard winds,
with flat-topped,
blue-green thatch,
and sun-catching orange limbs —

dark, secretive pine,
dipped in subconscious,
in glacial melt,
you shelter our dreams
inside a hay camp of needles;

with fruits, hard, green,
tipped to the sun,
a regiment of samurai,
splintering open.

Magnificent, noble pine,
statuesque,
contemplative,
nostalgically-hued,
a sticky sap weeps
from your invisible wounds.

Crows

Five a.m.
and the crows are up.
Their metallic caws
rip strips out of the sky.

Their caws,
which are older
than human ears,
are the callings of the future.

Reflected in their black eyes
globules of sun
fizz on cracked tarmac,
singed treetops bay.

Instinct tells them
one day
all this will be theirs:
their kingdom come.

A farmer's son

His name was Richard,
I remember that.
I used to run into him
as I was driving through the woods,
usually at first light—
I was a gamekeeper back then,
so this was my place of work.

I'd stop my Landrover
and we'd chat through the window,
mainly about the weather, I guess.
He always had a smile,
was well-spoken too,
and never did me any harm, camping out
in the woods as he did.

Over time, I found out his father
had owned a farm nearby,
but facing bankruptcy,
had hooked up the exhaust
of his old Volvo estate
and gassed himself.
His wife too.

Richard had one older brother,
who'd emigrated to Australia.
Rather bizarrely, it was his brother's wish
the Volvo be shipped out to him in Aus.
Quite why was anyone's guess.
That left Richard, sleeping rough in the woods.
I guess he'd come home.

I got him to come beating for me on shoot days,
paid him twenty quid like everyone else.
He was always happy to turn up
and was friendly with the guests.
He smelt though—
there was no getting away from that.
A stench that could have stained your walls.

I liked him though, for what it's worth.
I guess by today's standards
you'd say his mental health wasn't good.
Still, he got on with it, lived a life,
with a smile, as best he could
before he died one year in the cold.
I don't suppose he was very old.

The manure heap

It was at the end of a track,
banked up to a line of trees,
like some ancient burial mound
or unearthed mammoth.

Steam rose from its straw clumps,
like heat off a sodden fleece.
Wagtails flitted between
body-shaped mounds,

as effluent pooled,
bitumen thick,
like thawing blood.
Then at one end,

caked in muck,
a wind-snapped ash
resembled tusks,
where crows sat

watching shade-lines
chase across fields,
seamed with chalk.
Few came this way.

The field pond

I was warned
not to go near the edge,
that I would sink and
never come up if I did.
Who knew what was down there, my mother said.
But I didn't listen.

I waded in the shallows
of ancient leaf mould,
dragging up sticks
the length of crocodiles,
just as I climbed overhanging trees
and dangled my feet

over my reflection's
sunless gleam
where algae swirled
like dust in outer space
and leaves floated up
like corpses.

The birth

With shirtsleeves rolled high
over unsunned biceps
and arms gel-lubed, the vet
pats the cow's rump
and offers comforting words
before he begins.

The cow, looking back
over a scaffold of pin bones,
bellows a compliant,
but pained groan — the vet,
head turned, arm at full stretch,
inside her now, grimacing, as he straightens
her calf's twisted leg and pulls.

The cow's moans
are tremors through the bowels
of the earth, her sides
vacuumed inward
with the embryonic slop
of birth — the calf lands
outstretched, mucus-wet,
with soft yellow hooves.

The vet kneels, cradles
its floppy head
and rubs with straw.
The calf splutters; breathes.
The mother's rasp-rough tongue
soon at work, as we
stand back and watch

the calf's sprung ears,
eye blinks and attempts to stand,
but slipping, as if on ice,
before splay-legged,
collapsing in a heap.
Until finally — with encouraging
head-butts from mum — it stands.

Shoot Day

An estate wall —
flints snapped and coursed —
a steep-sided valley —
a convoy of 4x4s —

men with guns
stood at pegs,
the echo of sticks
and dogs —

a pheasant lifts
with centurion crow
and glides
over the valley rim.

For a moment,
nothing seems
more magnificent,
more sublime —

eyes lift,
the aesthetic freeze-framed.
When a gun goes up
and shots resound,

the bird's head
snaps back; wings fold.
And with final
synaptic charge,

gliding, it arcs,
wind-slicked, comet-tailed,
making death
somehow an art.

On my way to work

Sunrise. The flapping
of corrugated iron sheets.
I stop to open a gate

where cattle lumber
round a hayrack
in a fog of body heat.

Shoulder to shoulder,
tonguing frost off the metalwork,
nostrils flecked with hayseed,

they stare, jostling;
the earth's turning
in their pale-lashed eyes,

the axial tilt
in their knee bends.
With planetary stillness

they watch me,
as time lags
and frost-melt runs.

After heavy rain

Ditch water floods a gateway,
submerging fence posts
and spews over the bank sides —
the culvert blocked.

A raft of sticks, half-sucked in,
dams up its opening with leaves.
The water, regurgitating, foams sickly.
A faded crisp packet snags on barbwire.

The wind swirls.
Last night's rain drips from twigs.
I straddle the ditch, screwing
together drain rods, getting wet.

Done for the day

Late afternoon. The distant drone
of traffic along the A272.
I turn in a bonfire, smoke trails
across fields, sheep-tracked and muddied.

A crow, missing wing feathers,
caws down a gun-barrel sky.
Trees stand horizon back-lit —
brittle, bleached, overexposed.

The wind shifts, unsunned.
Thorn cuts smart on the backs of my hands.
I load up my chainsaw and fuel cans
and head home; done for the day.

The sound of snow

The snow was heavy that year.
It took the neighbour's 4x4
to get us up to the house.
You were downstairs —
the dining room, your new bedroom.
It'd been a while since you'd
remembered our names,
now your eyes were closed.

We sat with you,
sometimes together, sometimes alone.
There was no timetable.
Your breathing filled the house,
the walls your lungs now.
For three days, you kept it up.
A strong heart, they said.

We'd said goodnight, gone to bed,
when mum called us —
It's dad, come quickly.
And huddled round,
we held your hands, listening
as your breathing slowed,
until the only sound that night
was the sound of snow.

Ditching with cows for company

They stand and watch,
half-circling me,
bystanders to my work.
Then when my back is turned,

they move in, stealth mode —
sunken heads, telescopic necks —
and the next thing I know
is the heavy, shortened breaths,

the wet nostril touch —
a bashful first kiss —
a tonnage of clumsiness —
before finally,

as if permission were granted,
the abrasive, salty lick
to seal things off:
friends, I guess.

Philip Bentall is a novelist, poet and country estate worker. After studying countryside management, he worked as a gamekeeper in Sussex for several years before moving to London and doing a master's degree in Applied Linguistics at King's College. Writing his thesis on the influence of English on the Japanese language, he went on to teach Academic English to foundation and pre-master's students.

His poetry has received various awards and appeared in such publications as *The London Library Magazine* and *Country Life*. He is also the author of two novels, *Stray Dog* and *Wild Flower*. He lives in the south-east of England where he works as a country estate worker.

If you have enjoyed and appreciated this book, perhaps you would like to leave a review on Dempsey & Windle's website (www.dempseyandwindle/contact-us) or, if you bought it elsewhere, on the seller's website.